Take up

UPHOLSTERY

Take up UPHOLSTERY

LINDA FLANNERY & JANE McDONALD

KÖNEMANN

To Gordon and Aidan

Published in 1995 by
Merehurst Limited
Ferry House, 51 – 57 Lacy Road
Putney, London SW 15 1PR

Edited by Heather Dewhurst
Designed by Kit Johnson
Photography by Jon Bouchier
Illustrations by Paul Bryant
Key diagram by
King & King Design Associates

Typesetting by
Litho Link Limited, Welshpool, Powys
Colour seperation by
Fotographics Ltd,
UK – Hong Kong

Copyright © 1999 for this edition
Könemann Verlagsgesellschaft mbH
Bonner Str. 126, D- 50968 Cologne

Production Manager: Detlev Schaper
Assistants: Nicola Leurs, Alexandra Kiesling
Printing and Binding:
Sing Cheong Printing Co Ltd., Hong Kong
Printed in Hong Kong China

ISBN 3-8290-2989-6
10 9 8 7 6 5 4 3 2 1

Contents

UPHOLSTERY is something many people are nervous about, and wouldn't have a clue how to start. In fact it is surprisingly simple to do once you have mastered the basic techniques. This book guides beginners through the techniques of webbing, stuffing, stitching and buttoning, and demonstrates how to upholster chairs, stools and even a chaise longue, enabling you to update your furniture with fabrics of your choice and save money too. Upholstery is very satisfying – have a go with the help of this book and you will soon be sitting comfortably!

TOOLS & MATERIALS

*Tools used in upholstery are relatively simple to use
and fairly inexpensive to buy. In the beginning you may be
able to make do with similar tools that you already have, but as
you progress you will probably find it worthwhile
investing in the real thing.*

Listed on these two pages and illustrated overleaf are the tools and materials used for the various projects in this book. They should all be readily available from your local upholsterer. Once you have purchased your upholstery tools, do take care of them. Store them in a bag or box, and in an accessible place. Then you will be able to keep track of them and lay your hands on them as and when you need them. Before starting any of the projects in the book, check that you have all the tools and materials you will need. There is nothing more guaranteed to put you off finishing a project than being unable to find a particular needle when you need it, or running out of tacks or fibre stuffing in the middle of upholstering!

TOOLS

RIPPING CHISEL
This is used with a mallet to remove tacks. There are various types available but we have found those with a cranked shaft the most useful.

MALLET
Any type of carpenter's mallet is suitable. It is used together with a ripping chisel to remove tacks.

SCISSORS
Ideally, you should have two pairs of scissors – cutting-out shears for cutting fabric and small, pointed trimmers for snipping threads.

TACK LIFTER
This is mainly used for removing temporary tacks, but is also a useful tool for stripping.

WEBB STRETCHER
This tool is vital for stretching webbing across the frame of a chair. We have used a 'slot and peg' type.

MAGNETIC HAMMER
This is an upholsterer's hammer with two heads, one of which is magnetic and is used to pick up tacks.

REGULATOR
This is a large, flat-ended needle used to move stuffing around. The flat end is used for tucking fabric into narrow places. Take great care when handling a regulator, as the pointed end is very sharp. Cover the point with a cork when not in use.

NEEDLES
Spring: This is slightly curved and has a bayonet point for sewing through webbing.
Semi-circular: For the projects we have used 7.5cm (3in) and 10cm (4in) mattress needles and a 7.5cm (3in) cording needle.
Double pointed: This has a point at each end and is used for blind stitching, stay stitching and stitching a rolled edge. The most useful size is 25cm (10in). Take great care with a double pointed needle and keep the points covered when not in use.

PINS AND SKEWERS
Upholsterer's pins are heavier and longer than dressmaker's pins. Skewers are 10cm (4in) long with a looped end.

TAILOR'S CHALK
This is invaluable for marking top cover fabric as it can be rubbed away afterwards.

TAPE MEASURE
Steel or soft measures are available. You will find it useful to have both.

TACKS
These are readily available in various sizes, both 'improved' and 'fine'. Improved tacks have a heavier head.

GIMP PINS
These very fine tacks are available in several colours to match top cover fabric and braid or gimp.

STITCHING TWINE
This comes in various sizes and quality but we recommend you use a good quality – the twine used in this book is No.2.

LAID CORD
This is stout twine used for lashing springs.

SPRINGS
Coil springs are used in traditional upholstery and come in a variety of sizes and gauges. Zigzag springs are more modern and are fixed to the frame with special clips.

WAXED OR BUTTON THREAD
This is available in a variety of colours. It is stronger than unwaxed thread.

MATERIALS

WEBBING
There are two types: black and white, and jute webbing. Black and white is the stronger of the two.

HESSIAN
The most common weights used are 315g (10oz) and 375g (12oz), depending on the job in hand.

SCRIM HESSIAN
This is a loosely woven type of hessian and is used to cover the first layer of stuffing before stitching.

BLACK FIBRE AND HORSEHAIR
Black fibre is a coarse vegetable fibre used for first stuffing, and can also be used for second stuffing if horsehair is not readily available. We have used black fibre for both first and second stuffing as horsehair can be very expensive.

LINTERFELT AND BLACK COTTONFELT
Black cottonfelt is an inferior version of linterfelt. Linterfelt is softer, finer and should always be used as a top layer. It is available in the width of 67.5cm (27in) which is suitable for most projects.

POLYESTER WADDING (BATTING)
This is a man-made fibre available in various weights. We have used 60g (2oz), 125g (4oz) and 280g (9oz).

CALICO
This is an unbleached cotton used for a final covering before the top cover. Calico is available in various widths, any of which are suitable.

BOTTOM CLOTH
Similar to calico but of lesser quality, bottom cloth is used for covering the underside of furniture. It is available in various widths, all of which are suitable.

PIPING CORD
This is cotton cord which can be used for adding a decorative trim to seat covers and cushions.

FOAM
All foam must be flame retardant.

BRAID AND GIMP
These are used for final decoration. Braid has straight edges; gimp has a scalloped edge and is easier to fit around corners than braid.

TOP COVERS
There are many different types and qualities of upholstery fabric available for you to choose from. Before buying any, it is a good idea to seek advice from your local upholstery shop as to the suitability of various fabrics. All fabric used for upholstery must be flame retardant.

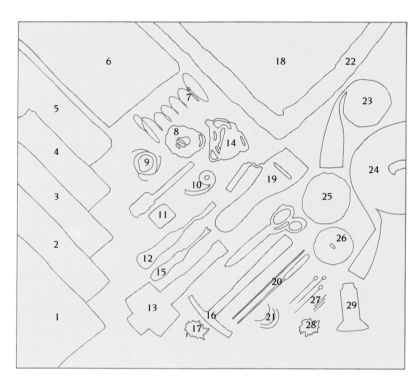

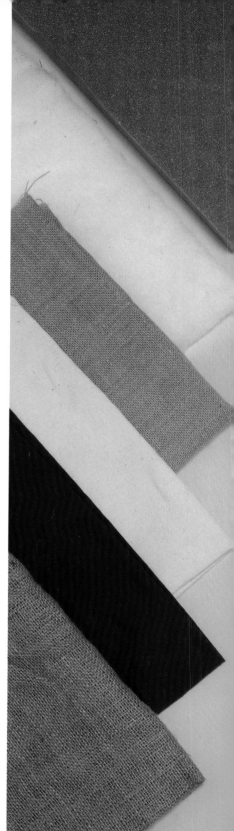

TOOLS AND EQUIPMENT

1. 315g (10oz) hessian
2. Bottom cloth
3. Calico
4. Scrim hessian
5. 60g (2oz) polyester wadding (batting)
6. Foam
7. Coil springs
8. Piping cord
9. Waxed thread
10. Tape measures
11. Tailor's chalk
12. Ripping chisel
13. Mallet
14. Braid
15. Tack lifter
16. Magnetic hammer
17. Tacks
18. Polyester wadding (batting)
19. Webb stretcher
20. Regulator and double pointed needle
21. Mattress needles
22. Linterfelt
23. Jute webbing
24. Black and white webbing
25. Laid cord
26. Stitching twine
27. Skewers and pins
28. Gimp pins
29. Button thread

STRIPPING & PREPARING THE FRAME

Before you can start to re-upholster a piece of furniture,
you will need to remove the existing upholstery and check the
condition of the frame.

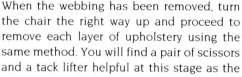

Once you have decided on the piece of furniture you want to re-upholster, stand back and take a good look at it. Remember how it looks and make a note as you are stripping how the layers have been built up. It is very unlikely that you will be able to re-use any of the materials except the horsehair which will need to be washed and dried. (The easiest way to do this is to put the horsehair in an old pillowcase and wash it by hand. Then lay it out in the sun to dry.)

Stripping the upholstery

Turn the piece upside-down and start by removing the bottom cloth which covers the webbing. Rest the blade of a ripping chisel against the first tack head and hit the wooden handle with a mallet. As the tack begins to lift, lower the handle of the chisel and continue to drive, but more gently, until the tack is removed. Take care when removing tacks near the show wood (polished wood). Make sure you watch the tack being removed and not the handle of the chisel, and keep your face away from the piece of furniture – tacks can fly! Then remove the webbing in the same way. Try always to work with the grain of the wood to avoid too much damage. This job can be a dusty and dirty one so do wear a mask.

It is almost impossible to strip a chair without splitting small pieces of wood from the frame. Save the fragments and, once the chair is stripped, stick them back with wood glue.

When the webbing has been removed, turn the chair the right way up and proceed to remove each layer of upholstery using the same method. You will find a pair of scissors and a tack lifter helpful at this stage as the work becomes more fiddly. Remember to keep a record of the layers of material as you strip them, as this will serve as a reminder when you come to re-upholstering later.

Preparing the frame

Once the upholstery has been stripped off, check the condition of the bare frame. If there is any evidence of live woodworm (fine sawdust falling from the frame) treat the wood with a proprietary woodworm killer (follow the instructions on the can). Fill all tack holes with a mixture of wood glue and sawdust – spread a fairly stiff mixture over the surface, making sure each hole is filled. You do not need to sand or varnish the wood afterwards as this part of the frame will not be visible once you have completed the upholstery.

If the frame is in a poor condition, for example showing signs of splintering or cracking, soak strips of hessian in wood glue and then wrap them around the frame. If any of the joints have become loose or broken you will need to take the chair to your local antique restorer or carpenter to be repaired before you can start to re-upholster.

◆ *Stripping a frame (right)*

CROSS-SECTION OF CHAIR SEAT

REMOVING WEBBING

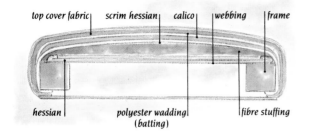

top cover fabric | scrim hessian | calico | webbing | frame

hessian | polyester wadding (batting) | fibre stuffing

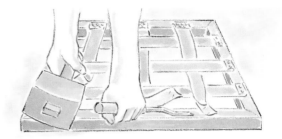

◆ When stripping a piece of furniture, keep a note of how the layers have been built up. This will be helpful when you re-upholster the piece.

◆ Rest the blade of a ripping chisel against a tack head and hit the wooden handle with a mallet. Lower the handle of the chisel as the tack begins to lift. Repeat with the tacks all around the chair frame to remove the webbing.

Webbing

*Webbing forms the basic support for all
upholstery so it is vital to get it right! Follow these instructions
for perfect webbing.*

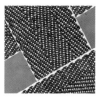

First find the centre of the frame from back to front and from side to side and mark with a pencil. You will then need to work out the number of webbs required to fill the frame, allowing for a gap of approximately 5cm (2in) between each piece. Starting on your centre mark and working from back to front, attach your first piece of webbing to the back rail of the frame. Turn over 2.5cm (1in) of the end of a roll of webbing and, using a magnetic hammer, tack this to the back rail using five 13mm improved tacks in a W-shape. This will help prevent the wood from splitting. For heavier furniture, use 16mm improved tacks.

Take the webb stretcher and, with the handle of the stretcher pointing towards the chair, push a loop of webbing through the hole of the stretcher from underneath. Place the stretcher bar through the loop. Stretch the webbing over the front rail at the centre and pull the handle firmly towards you. Hammer three 13mm improved tacks in a V-shape through the stretched webbing 2.5cm (1in) from the row of tacks. Fold the webbing back on itself and hammer in two more tacks between the ones underneath.

Then attach the side-to-side webbs to the frame. Take the loose webbing and weave it over and under the existing webbing and attach as before, using five 13mm improved tacks for each webb.

◆ *Webbing a frame (below)*

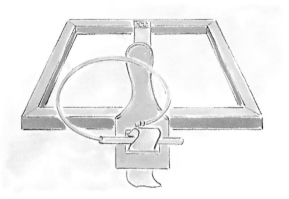

1 ◆ Turn over 2.5cm (1in) of the end of a roll of webbing and tack this to the centre of the back rail of the frame by hammering in five 13mm improved tacks in a W-shape.

2 ◆ With the handle of the webb stretcher pointing towards the frame, push a loop of webbing through the hole in the stretcher from underneath. Place the stretcher bar through the loop.

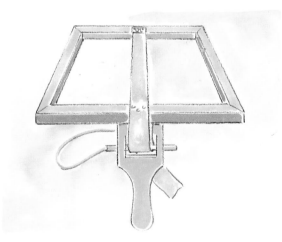

3 ◆ Stretch the webbing over the front rail of the frame at the centre and pull the handle of the webb stretcher towards you. Hammer three 13mm improved tacks in a V-shape through the webbing. Fold the webbing back on itself and hammer in two more tacks between the ones underneath.

4 ◆ To attach the side-to-side webbs, weave the loose webbing over and under the existing webbing and tack to each side of the frame as before.

Hessian &
Bridle Stitches

Hessian is used to cover the webbing and support the stuffing.
Once you have made bridle stitches in the hessian, then the fibre
stuffing can be added.

Attaching the hessian

Cut a piece of 315g (10oz) or 375g (12oz) hessian about 5cm (2in) larger than you need to cover your webbed or sprung frame. Turn up about a 2.5cm (1in) hem along the back rail of the frame and attach the hessian to the centre of the rail using the hammer and 13mm tacks. (Use improved tacks for heavier frames and fine tacks for lighter frames.) Only temporary tack at this stage, making sure that the hessian remains square. Pull the hessian towards you across the frame and tack it directly opposite the first tack. Put a tack in the centre of the other two rails in the same way. Pull the hessian tight from corner to corner, securing each corner with a tack. Now place tacks about 5cm (2in) apart between those already in the frame. When your hessian is square and tight, hammer the tacks home firmly. Trim the hessian, turn up the hem and tack down in between the existing tacks.

◆ *Attaching hessian to the frame (right)*

ATTACHING HESSIAN

1 ◆ Cut a piece of hessian about 5cm (2in) larger than the frame. Turn up a 2.5cm (1in) hem and temporary tack the hessian to the back rail. Pull the hessian towards you and tack it opposite the first tack.

2 ◆ Tack the hessian to the centre of the other two rails. Then secure each corner with a tack and place extra tacks 5cm (2in) apart between the skeleton tacks in the frame.

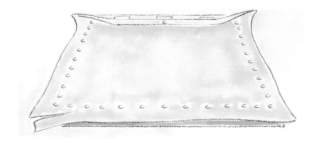

3 ◆ Using scissors, carefully and neatly trim the hessian approximately 4cm (1½ in) outside the tacks.

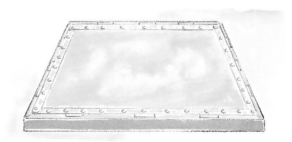

4 ◆ Turn up the hem all the way around the frame and tack down, making sure you tack in between the existing tacks. The hessian should now be neatly secured to the frame.

1 ◆ Using a needle threaded with twine, push the needle through the hessian and back out again, so you have two pieces of twine visible.

2 ◆ Hold the two protruding pieces of twine between thumb and forefinger so they are taut.

3 ◆ Loop the right piece of twine over the left piece while still holding both lengths taut.

4 ◆ Wrap the right piece of twine around both lengths twice, then bring it out to the right, through the loop created in step 2.

5 ◆ Pull the twine tight so that the loops bunch up to make a knot.

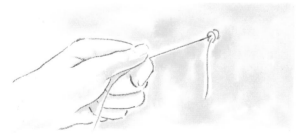

6 ◆ Let go of the right piece of twine and pull the left piece. The knot will slide back to the hessian.

Making bridle stitches

Thread a spring needle with enough twine to make taut ties in several lines across the frame. Starting in the top left-hand corner of the frame, make an upholsterer's knot (see opposite). Working your way backwards and forwards across the frame, make large stitches. These bridle stitches will hold your stuffing in place. Finish with an upholsterer's knot.

Stuffing with fibre

Tease out one handful of curly black fibre at a time. Tuck it under and around each bridle stitch. Work from the back of the frame to the front, tucking in fibre, packing it and pressing down firmly as you go. Make sure there are no gaps in the stuffing. The finished stuffed seat should feel firm and thick and be domed in shape.

MAKING BRIDLE STITCHES

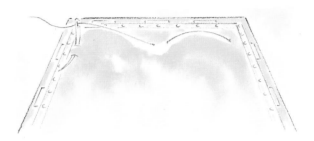

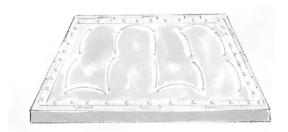

1 ◆ Using a spring needle and twine, make large running stitches forwards and backwards in straight lines across the hessian, starting in the top left-hand corner of the frame.

2 ◆ When the hessian is covered with large bridle stitches, secure the stitches with an upholsterer's knot and trim the end of the twine.

STUFFING WITH FIBRE

1 ◆ Tuck handfuls of curly black fibre under and around each bridle stitch. Work from the back of the frame to the front, tucking in the fibre and pressing it down firmly as you go.

2 ◆ Ensure there are no gaps in the stuffing. When you have finished, the stuffed seat should feel firm and thick and be domed in the centre.

SCRIM & STITCHING

*A layer of scrim hessian is used to cover
the fibre stuffing. The shape of the seat is then formed by stitching
through the scrim hessian.*

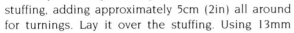

Attaching the scrim

Scrim hessian is a loose, woven type of hessian which can be moulded to cover stuffing. It is not used for covering springs. Cut a piece large enough to cover the stuffing, adding approximately 5cm (2in) all around for turnings. Lay it over the stuffing. Using 13mm improved tacks, temporary tack in three places on each rail. Make sure the hessian is taught and straight and that the stuffing feels firm underneath. If necessary, redistribute the stuffing using a regulator (see below). Cut for obstructions (see page 34). Working from the centre outwards, tack the hessian in place.

ATTACHING SCRIM HESSIAN

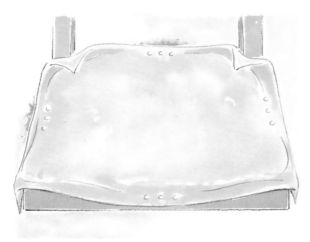

1 ♦ Cut a piece of scrim hessian large enough to cover the stuffing, with an allowance of 5cm (2in) all around. Lay it over the stuffing. Temporary tack the scrim hessian in three places on each rail with 13mm improved tacks.

2 ♦ Check that the scrim hessian is taut and straight and that the stuffing feels firm underneath. Cut for obstructions (see page 34) then, working from the centre outwards on each side, hammer in 13mm improved tacks along each rail of the frame.

Using a regulator

The regulator is one of the most useful tools an upholsterer has to hand. Its main use is to redistribute the stuffing within the scrim hessian to produce a desired shape. This is done by inserting the regulator a third of its length through the scrim into the stuffing. Then, using a circular movement, you will be able to 'regulate' and move the stuffing around within the scrim to fill any gaps.

Stay stitches

Thread a double pointed needle with stitching twine at least 2m (80in) long. Starting at approximately 10–15cm (4–6in) away from the edge of the seat, push the needle through the scrim and stuffing until it clears the hessian below. Then push the needle back up through the seat using the other pointed end of the needle. Make an upholsterer's knot (see page 18). Using large stitches, stab the needle through the hessian and stuffing and back again in the same way, making a row of large stitches parallel to the edge of the seat. This line of stay stitches will hold the stuffing firm and in place while you make your stitched edge. Then turn up the scrim and neatly tack between the first row of tacks all around the seat. Trim off the excess scrim.

REGULATING THE STUFFING

◆ Push the regulator a third of its length through the scrim into the stuffing. Then move it around in a circular motion to distribute the stuffing within the scrim. In this way you can fill any air pockets in the stuffing and make it evenly compact. Keep checking for any gaps in the stuffing as you distribute it around within the scrim.

STAY STITCHING

◆ Using a double pointed needle threaded with 2m (80in) of stitching twine, push the needle through the scrim and stuffing about 10–15cm (4–6in) from the edge of the seat. Then bring the needle back through the scrim and stuffing using the other pointed end of the needle to make the first stitch. Make an upholsterer's knot (see page 18) to secure the thread. Then make a row of long running stitches in the same way all around the seat and parallel to the edge. This line of stay stitches will keep the stuffing in position and densely packed.

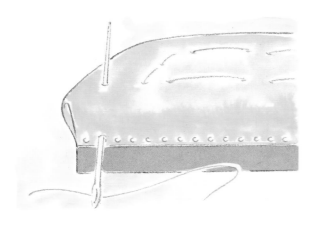

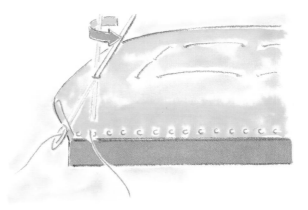

1 ◆ Thread a double pointed needle with stitching twine three times the circumference of the seat. Working from left to right, push the needle into the seat about 2.5cm (1in) from the left corner, just above the line of tacks. Bring the point of the needle out through the top of the scrim approximately 10cm (4in) from the edge of the seat.

2 ◆ Begin to pull the needle through the seat. When the lower point enters the seat, twist the needle anticlockwise and push it back down so that it emerges at the corner of the seat.

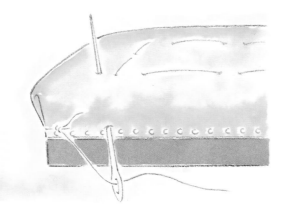

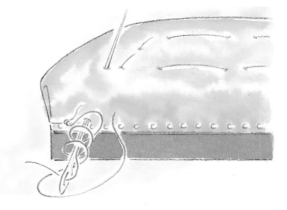

3 ◆ Make an upholsterer's knot (see page 18) and pull it tight to secure the twine. Insert the needle 4cm (1½in) to the right of the knot. Using a circular movement as before, push the needle back down through the stuffing so that it protrudes halfway.

4 ◆ Take the twine leading from the knot and wind it around the needle three times. Then pull the needle towards you and pin it in the scrim to anchor it, while you tighten the stitch with short tugs.

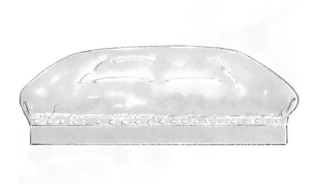

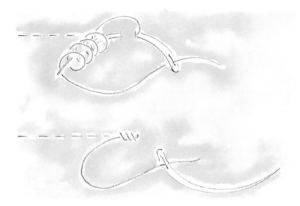

5 ◆ Continue stitching in this way around the seat, regulating as you go to draw the stuffing to the edge. A seat will usually require two rows of blind stitching. The rows should be 1.5cm (⅝in) apart.

◆ When making the last stitch, and before you pull the needle through the fabric, wind the thread around the end of the needle three or four times. Then pull the needle through the loops to tighten the knot. Make two more small running stitches to stop the knot coming undone before cutting the thread.

Blind stitching

To make a stitched edge around your seat, first cut a piece of stitching twine three times the circumference of the seat. Then, working from left to right using a double pointed needle, push your threaded needle into the stuffed seat just above the line of tacks and about 2.5cm (1in) from the left-hand corner. The point of your needle should come through the top of the scrim approximately 10cm (4in) from the edge of the seat. Before the needle comes right through the scrim, twist it anticlockwise and push it back down so that it emerges at the starting point. Make an upholsterer's knot (see page 18) and pull it tight.

The circular movement of the needle ensures that the fibre stuffing is drawn towards the edge of the seat as you stitch. Insert the needle again 4cm (1½in) away from the knot. Using the same circular movement as before, push the needle back down through the stuffing so that the needle protrudes

halfway through. Take the twine leading from the knot and wind it clockwise around the needle three times. Then pull the needle right through towards you and pin it in the scrim to anchor it while you tighten the stitch with short tugs.

Continue stitching in this way around the seat, regulating as you go to draw the stuffing to the edge. Finish off the row of blind stitches with either a granny knot or a French knot. Always finish a French knot by making two more stitches before cutting the twine – this will stop it coming undone.

A seat will usually need two rows of blind stitching around the edge before you make the rolled edge with topstitching. Each row of blind stitches should be worked approximately 1.5cm (⅝in) above the last. Take care to regulate the stuffing enough at each corner of the seat to produce the right angle. The stuffing should be firm and densely packed, with no hollows or air pockets.

Topstitching

The final row of stitching will form a firm edge to the seat, ensuring that it keeps its shape. These stitches are very like blind stitches but the needle is pulled right through the stuffing to form a line of stitches on either side of a roll. Cut a piece of twine four times the circumference of the seat. Work from left to right once more and regulate between each stitch. Insert the needle about 2.5cm (1in) from the edge of the seat, as if you were about to make a blind stitch at an angle of about 45° but this time pull it right through the scrim. Take the needle back down again at the corner, finishing the stitch off as you would a blind stitch. Continue on around the seat and finish with a French knot (see page 23). You should now have a strong, firm edge to the seat.

◆ *Topstitching a seat (below) and a chair with scrim hessian stitched in place (right)*

1 ◆ Insert a double pointed needle threaded with stitching twine into the seat about 2.5cm (1in) in from the corner and at an angle of 45°. Pull the needle right through the scrim, then take it back down again at the corner. Finish the stitch off by winding the thread around the needle three times. Continue making stitches in the same way around the edge of the seat.

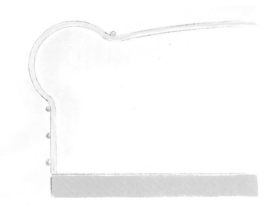

2 ◆ When you have finished the row of stitching, make a French knot (see page 23). There will now be a line of stitches on either side of a roll, forming a strong, firm edge.

SECOND STUFFING, LINTERFELT & CALICO

*On top of the scrim the upholstery layers are built
up further with a second fibre stuffing, two layers of linterfelt
and a layer of calico.*

Second stuffing

Having stitched your rolled edge you will find that the centre of the seat will be somewhat depressed. You will now need to stuff the seat again. Make another set of

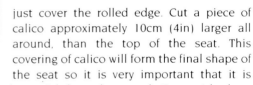

bridle stitches (see page 19) but this time make them shallower and tighter. Insert a layer of teased black fibre about 2.5cm (1in) thick under and around the bridles. Make sure that the stuffing does not cover the rolled edge. The seat should now be slightly domed in shape.

Linterfelt and calico

You will need to place at least two layers of linterfelt over the second stuffing, the first layer slightly smaller than the second. The second layer should

just cover the rolled edge. Cut a piece of calico approximately 10cm (4in) larger all around, than the top of the seat. This covering of calico will form the final shape of the seat so it is very important that it is pulled down tightly and secured. Start with three temporary tacks in the centre of each rail. Then, working from the centre outwards on each side, temporary tack all around and cut for obstructions (see page 34). These temporary tacks can be removed and replaced as you work around again, smoothing the calico as you go. Finish the corners neatly (see page 36). When the calico is tight enough, hammer the temporary tacks home and trim the excess calico.

◆ *Second stuffing a chair (right)*

SECOND STUFFING

◆ Make a set of tight bridle stitches (see page 19) on top of the scrim hessian. Insert a layer of teased black fibre about 2.5cm (1in) thick under and around the bridles and pack tightly to give the seat a slightly domed shape. Ensure that the stuffing does not cover the rolled edge.

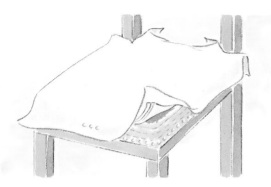

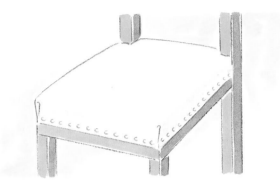

1 ◆ Place two layers of linterfelt over the second stuffing before attaching the calico. Cut a piece of calico 10cm (4in) larger all around than the top of the seat. Lay it over the linterfelt and temporary tack in the centre of each rail of the frame. Then cut for obstructions (see page 34).

2 ◆ Working from the centre outwards, temporary tack all around the frame. Then work around the frame again to smooth and tighten the calico, removing and replacing the tacks as you go. Finish the corners neatly. When the calico is tight, hammer the temporary tacks home and trim off the excess calico.

WADDING, TOP COVER & BRAID

Polyester wadding (batting) and the top cover are the
two final layers of an upholstered seat. All you need to add then is
a braid or gimp trim for a finishing touch.

Wadding (batting) and top cover

Before the top cover is put on you will need to place a layer of polyester wadding (batting) on the surface to be covered. This will give the top cover a good surface to bed into and help prevent wear of the fabric. After attaching the layer of calico, cut a piece of wadding (batting) just a little smaller than the top cover fabric and lay it on the calico surface.

The top cover fabric should be put on in much the same way as the calico but do make sure that it is lying square and any pattern is centred. To do this, mark the centre of each side of the fabric with a nick and the centre of the rails with chalk and, when tacking in place, match the marks up.

◆ *Tacking the top cover in position (below)*

Attaching the braid or gimp

To cover the raw edge of the trimmed top cover fabric, you will need a suitable braid or gimp. There are numerous colours and designs to choose from. To attach the braid, turn the end of the braid under approximately 12mm (½in) and secure it at one end with two gimp pins. Holding the braid taut, spread fabric adhesive along the underside, about 10cm (4in) at a time. Place the braid over the tacks, pressing it firmly as you go so it sticks to the surface. To finish off, cut the braid with 12mm (½in) to spare, turn this under and secure with two more gimp pins.

ATTACHING THE TOP COVER

◆ Lay the top cover fabric over the wadding (batting), ensuring that any pattern is centred. Tack the fabric securely in place, positioning the tacks close to the show wood. Trim the fabric just below the tacks to leave a raw edge.

ATTACHING BRAID

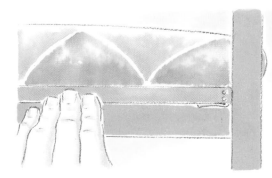

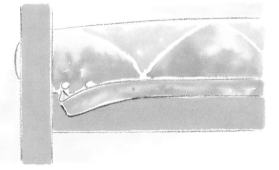

1 ◆ Turn under one end of the braid by approximately 12mm (½in) and secure at one end of the seat with two gimp pins. Spread fabric adhesive along 10cm (4in) of the underside of the braid. Press the braid over the raw edge of the top cover and hold in place for a few seconds until it is secure.

2 ◆ Continue applying fabric adhesive along 10cm (4in) sections and holding the braid in place all around the seat. To finish off, trim the end of the braid leaving 12mm (½in) spare. Turn this under and secure in place with two more gimp pins.

Stylish Summery Stripes

Brighten up a drop-in seat with these colourful stripes. This simple project uses several of the basic upholstery techniques and will help to build your confidence and give you plenty of practice using the tools before you progress onto a more complicated project.

SIZE

Finished seat cover measures 40cm (16in) wide and 47cm (18¾in) long.

YOU WILL NEED

3m (5¾yd) webbing

13mm improved tacks

50cm (20in) of 315g (10oz) hessian

Stitching twine

750g (1½lb) black fibre

1m (40in) linterfelt

60cm (24in) calico

10mm fine tacks

50cm (20in) polyester wadding (batting)

60cm (24in) top cover fabric

50cm (20in) bottom cloth

Making up

1 ◆ For this project you will find it easiest to work on a flat surface, such as a sturdy table or work bench. Strip all materials and tacks from the seat and prepare the frame as on pages 12–13.

2 ◆ Starting with the empty frame, webb the seat using six strips of webbing (three on each side) and 13mm improved tacks.

3 ◆ Attach the hessian over the webbing as on page 16, making sure that the hessian covers the webbing but is not too near the edge of the seat.

4 ◆ Make several shallow bridle stitches and space them apart (see page 19).

5 ◆ Stuff the seat as on page 19, keeping the stuffing well away from the edges. The stuffing should be a lot firmer in the middle of the seat than around the edges.

6 ◆ Lay two layers of linterfelt over the stuffing – the first layer should

be 5cm (2in) smaller than the frame and the second layer should be large enough to reach the edge of the frame but not go over the sides (see page 26).

7 ◆ Cut a piece of calico 4cm (1½in) larger than the frame and lay it on the linterfelt. Now, holding the frame, stuffing and calico in two hands, turn the whole seat upside-down. It may be easier for you to replace temporary tacks on each side before you do this.

8 ◆ Pulling the calico over the front rail, temporary tack with 10mm fine tacks into the centre of the rail. Now go to the back rail and pull the calico tightly towards you and temporary tack again in the centre of the back rail. Repeat on the side rails.

9 ◆ Going to each corner in turn, lift the seat slightly from the bench and pull the calico tight over the corner towards you. Use the other hand to smooth and compress the stuffing underneath. Hammer a tack into the centre of each corner. Working from the centre of each rail outwards, temporary tack the calico towards the corner.

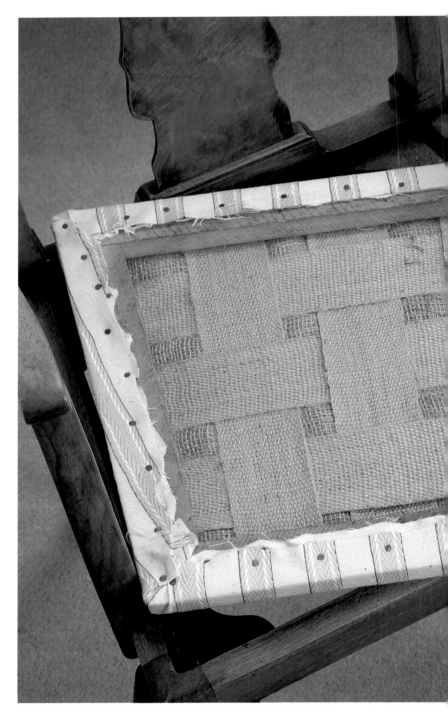

◆ *Compressing the stuffing*

10 ♦ To neaten the corners of the calico, make two slits towards each corner and cut away excess calico. Fold over both side edges of the fabric to enclose the corner piece and tack the calico in position. Trim close to the tacks along all edges. Hammer the tacks home when the calico is tight enough and trim again.

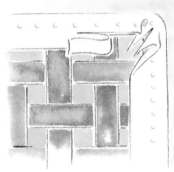

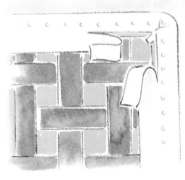

♦ *Trimming and folding the calico for a neatly finished corner*

11 ♦ Turn the frame the right way up. Cut out a piece of wadding (batting) exactly the same size as the top of the seat and lay it on top of the calico. Cut out a piece of top cover fabric 10cm (4in) larger than the frame and lay this over the wadding (batting). Holding these layers together, turn the seat upside-down again. Use a ruler or tape measure to find the centre of the fabric and the frame and mark with notches and pencil (see page 28). Match them together.

♦ *Marking and matching the centres of the fabric and the frame*

12 ♦ Attach the top cover in the same way as the calico and finish the corners neatly. Trim the excess fabric, leaving a raw edge. Now cover the bottom of the frame with bottom cloth and tack in position.

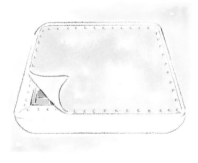

♦ *Attaching the bottom cloth*

CUTTING FOR OBSTRUCTIONS & CURVES

*To give your upholstery a really professional finish
you need to be able to cut correctly around any obstructions, such
as chair legs and curves. Here's how you do it.*

Cutting for obstructions

Lay your fabric on the surface to be covered, making sure that it is lying square and the pattern is centred. Fold the corners of the fabric back towards you and away from the obstruction to within approximately 1–3cm (½–1¼ in) of the wood. The distance here depends on the depth of the stuffing underneath. Cut diagonally from the corners to the obstruction, ending the cut with a small V-shape as shown opposite. The fabric should now fold down neatly around the obstruction without the cut being visible. Trim away the excess fabric at the corners to prevent it bunching and not lying flat.

CUTTING FOR OBSTRUCTIONS

 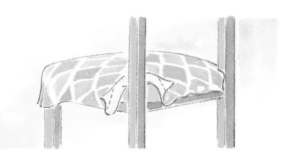

1 ◆ Lay the fabric on the seat, ensuring that it is lying square and that any pattern is centred. Fold the corners of the fabric away from the obstructions and towards the centre of the seat, to within 1–3cm (½–1¼ in) of the wood, depending on the depth of the stuffing. Cut diagonally from the corner of the fabric towards the obstruction, ending the cut with a small V-shape.

2 ◆ Fold the fabric back down around the obstruction. It should fold down neatly without the cut showing. Trim off the corners to prevent the fabric bunching, tucking the fabric down with a regulator.

◆ *Cutting for obstructions (right)*

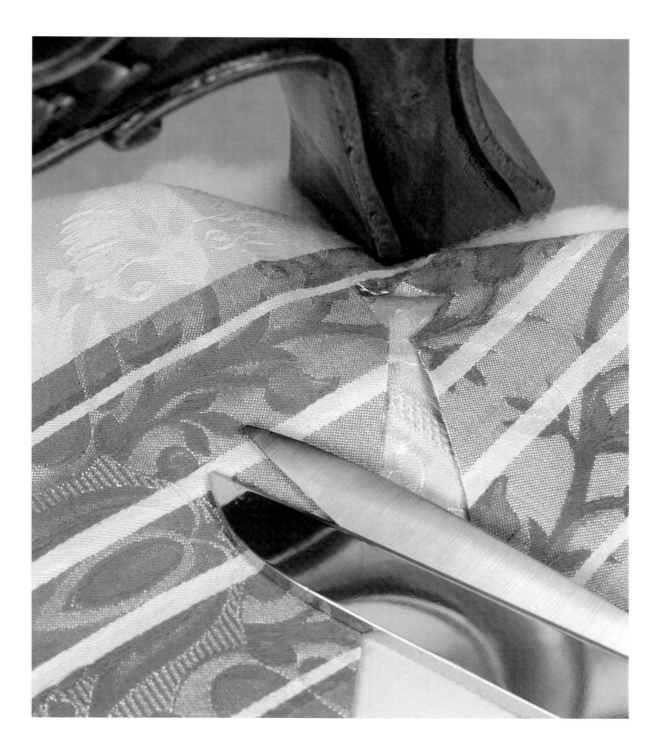

Cutting for corners and pleating

For square corners, fold the fabric to the left and tack down. Cut a slit next to the tacks and cut away excess fabric in a triangular shape. Take the folded fabric back over the tacks to make a pleat and tack.

For rounded corners, smooth the fabric over the corner and tack in place. Then cut away excess fabric in a small triangular shape on either side of the tacks. Fold the two side pieces of fabric back over the tacks to create two neat pleats, and tack to secure.

PLEATED SQUARE CORNERS

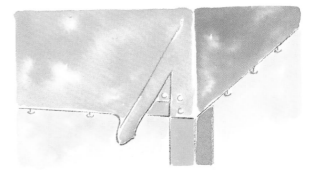

1 ◆ Fold the fabric to the left side of the corner. Place two tacks in the corner, one above the other, 2.5cm (1in) from the edge.

2 ◆ Cut a slit in the fabric alongside the tacks and cut away excess in a triangular shape. Bring the fabric back over the tacks to create a pleat. Tack in place.

PLEATED ROUNDED CORNERS

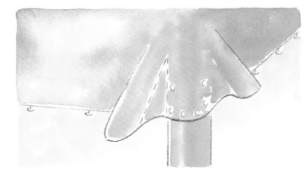

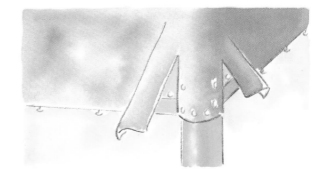

1 ◆ Fold the fabric straight over the corner so that it forms two 'wings' of excess fabric. Tack the fabric to the frame as shown.

2 ◆ Cut a slit in the fabric on each side of the tacks and cut away excess in a triangular shape. Fold the fabric 'wings' back over the tacks and tack down.

Cutting for a curve

It is useful to know this technique when tackling a curved obstruction such as at the base of the wing of a wing-backed armchair. Fold the fabric back towards you and away from the curve. Make several small cuts into the curve at approximately 1.5cm (⅝in) intervals. This will enable the fabric to lie smoothly around the curve. Depending on the stuffing underneath, end your cut approximately 1–2cm (½–¾in) from the curve.

CUTTING FOR A CURVE

◆ To enable the fabric to lie smooth and flat around a curve, fold the fabric away from the curve and cut several small notches into the curve with a pair of sharp, pointed scissors at approximately 1.5cm (⅝in) intervals. End the cut approximately 1–2cm (½–¾in) from the curve.

◆ Cutting for a curve (below)

WELL SCREENED

Add a touch of glamour to your room with this
upholstered screen. As the wood is easy to cut, you can make
the top of the panels any shape you like – arched,
rounded or even pointed.

SIZE

Finished screen measures
122cm (48½in) wide and
165cm (66in) high.

YOU WILL NEED

2m (2¼yd) top cover fabric,
137cm (54in) wide, for the
front

2m (2¼yd) contrasting top
cover fabric, 137cm (54in)
wide, for the back

3 panels of 2cm (¾in) MDF
board, cut to size and
shaped at the top

10.5m (12yd 2in) of 60g (2oz)
polyester wadding (batting)

Upholstery spray adhesive

10mm fine tacks

10–12m (11¼–13½yd)
braid or gimp, depending
on the size of the panels

Gimp pins

6 brass hinges and screws

For this project you will need the
help of your local carpenter or
wood yard. MDF is an ideal
material to use and can be cut to
any shape or size. The panels we
have used measure 42 × 170cm
(16¾ × 68in). This means that all
three panels can not only be cut
out of one width of fabric, but you
will also find it easier to line up
any pattern in the fabric. Choose a
fairly thin cotton fabric as a top
cover as it will be easier to
handle. Cotton chintz is an ideal
material, but it may need to be
flame retarded before you use it.

Making up

1 ◆ Lay each 2m (2¼yd) piece of
fabric on a flat surface and divide
each width into three equal
pieces. Mark the cutting lines with
chalk before you cut.

2 ◆ Lay the centre panel of MDF
board on a large flat surface. Cut
out a piece of polyester wadding
(batting) exactly the same size as
the MDF panel and place it on the
board. You can use a light coating
of upholstery spray adhesive to
keep the wadding (batting) in
place while you are tacking on the
top cover.

3 ◆ Take the centre piece of top
cover fabric and mark the centre
of this and the board, top and

bottom. Place the piece of fabric
on the wadding (batting) and
match the marks. Starting at the
top, place three 10mm fine tacks
in the top edge of the board. Now
move to the base, smoothing the
fabric as you go, pull tight and
place three temporary tacks in the
bottom edge, matching the marks.

Now finish temporary tacking the top and bottom edge before moving to the sides. If you have made your panel particularly curved at the top, you may need to cut into the curve (see below).

back of panel

◆ *Cutting the curve*

4 ◆ Now temporary tack the sides, working from the centre outwards on each side. Do not pull the fabric too tight at this stage as you may distort the pattern. Finish the corners as on page 36. When the fabric is taut, hammer the tacks home and trim the excess fabric close to the tacks.
5 ◆ Now turn the panel over, protecting the fabric underneath as necessary. Treat in exactly the same way, this time using your contrasting fabric. Try to place the tacks in between those on the first side so that you finish up with only one straight row of tacks. Trim the fabric close to the tacks, again leaving a raw edge.
6 ◆ Cover the tacks with braid or gimp no wider than the depth of board, that is, 2cm (¾ in) wide.
7 ◆ Finish the two remaining panels in the same way. Make sure you use the correct piece of fabric for each panel.
8 ◆ Join the three panels together with small brass hinges.

SWEET DREAMS

*This single upholstered headboard is an example
of modern upholstery with its use of foam for the base. Choose
a fabric to match your bedroom and make the
headboard as large as you like.*

SIZE

Finished headboard
measures 93cm (37¼in)
wide and 68cm (27¼in)
long.

YOU WILL NEED

1 piece of 2cm (¾in) MDF
board cut to exact size and
shape of headboard

1 piece of foam, 2.5cm (1in)
thick, the same size as the
headboard

Upholstery spray adhesive

1.5m (60in) of 60g (2oz)
polyester wadding (batting)

1.5m (60in) top cover fabric

10mm fine tacks

1m (40in) contrast piping
fabric

4m (4½yd) piping cord

Gimp pins

2m (2¼yd) black and white
webbing

70cm (28in) calico

2 pieces of 7.5 × 2.5cm (3 ×
1in) planed timber, 60cm
(24in) long

◆ *Different headboard shapes*

Ask your local carpenter to cut
the MDF board to the exact
shape and size of headboard
you require (see suggestions
above). You will also need to cut
slots 1cm (½in) wide and 20cm
(8in) long in the two pieces of
planed timber (see below).

Making up
1 ◆ Lay the board on a flat surface
and mark a line on the board with
chalk as shown below.
2 ◆ Cut a piece of foam the exact
size of the headboard. To do this,
place the board on top of the
foam and draw around the edge

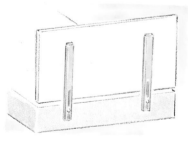

◆ *Back of headboard*

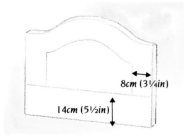

◆ *Marking the headboard*

with a felt-tip pen. Cut the foam along your line with a large pair of scissors, mark the foam in exactly the same way as the headboard and cut along the lines again with a large pair of scissors. Keep pieces 'A' and 'B' and discard 'C'.

3 ◆ Using upholstery spray adhesive, stick the piece of foam 'A' within your chalk line on the board. Cut a piece of polyester wadding (batting) the same size as 'A' and lay this over the foam.

4 ◆ Cut a piece of fabric 3cm (1¼in) larger than the foam and position it on the wadding (batting), centring any pattern and making sure it is lying square. Starting at the top, place three temporary tacks about 1cm (½in) beyond your chalk line on the board. Now go to the bottom and place three temporary tacks 1cm (½in) beyond your chalk line. Then repeat on both sides. Working from the centre outwards on each side, drawing the fabric away from you and towards the corners, tack the fabric all around with temporary tacks. When you are sure the fabric is taut, hammer the tacks home and trim the fabric to within 6mm (¼in) of the tacks.

5 ◆ Make up two lengths of piping in your contrast fabric. One piece should be about 2m (2¼yd) long and the other 1.6m (64in) long. Cut strips of fabric on the bias approximately 4–5cm (1½–2in) wide, depending on the thickness of piping cord used. To obtain the correct length, join each strip by matching the slanted edges (see below). To cover the cord fold the fabric over the cord and match the raw edges (see below). Machine stitch using a zip or piping foot as close to the cord as possible. Trim the raw edge to within 1cm (¼in) of the seam.

6 ◆ Place the shorter piece of piping over your line of tacks, lining up the raw edge of piping with the raw edge of trimmed fabric. Tack the piping on the board in this position, placing your tacks approximately 3cm (1¼in) apart. To ease the piping around the corners, make small nicks in the piping towards the seam.

7 ◆ Cut five widths of fabric 13cm (5¼in) wide and machine them together to make one long strip. Match the pattern if necessary. With the right sides of the fabric together, lay the border over the

piping, lining up all the raw edges. Starting in the bottom right-hand corner, anchor the border with one tack near the edge. Now make tiny pleats with the fabric no more than 1cm (½in) wide and secure each pleat with a gimp pin. Continue in this way around the whole length of piping cord (see below).

8 ◆ Take a piece of black and white webbing 2m (2¼yd) long, cut in half lengthways, and place one end over the raw edge of the border, butting the uncut edge of webbing as close as possible to the piping cord underneath. Tack the webbing in this position at frequent intervals around the gathered border. Place your tacks as close to the edge of the webbing as possible. Make cuts into the webbing to ease it around the corners. Cut off the excess webbing when you reach the other end. This is called backtacking.

9 ◆ Keeping the border folded back, use upholstery spray adhesive to stick the piece of foam 'B' in position. Cover this with polyester wadding (batting). Starting in the centre at the top, take the gathered border over the

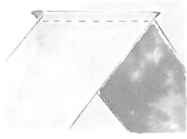

◆ Joining fabric for piping

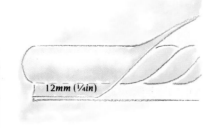

12mm (¼in)

◆ Covering piping cord

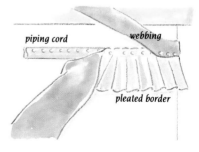

piping cord   webbing

pleated border

◆ Attaching the border and webbing

foam and wadding (batting) and over the back of the headboard. Tack down. Ease the pleats out as you go, taking care on the curves and at the corners.

10 ◆ Cut a piece of fabric large enough to cover area 'C' plus an allowance of 4cm (1½in) all around. Lay this piece over area 'A', with the wrong side uppermost, making sure the fabric is square and centred. Match the raw edge of 'A' with the raw edge of 'C', making sure that the edge of the gathered border is also covered. Place a few tacks along this line to hold the fabric in place, while backtacking the other half of your piece of webbing over the raw edge as for the gathered border.

11 ◆ Keeping the strip of fabric folded back, cover the area 'C' with two layers of polyester wadding (batting) before folding the fabric back over the wadding (batting) and tacking it to the back of the headboard. Finish the corners as shown on page 36.

12 ◆ Take your second piece of piping and tack it around the back of the headboard. The raw edge of piping should face inwards away from the edge. Tuck the ends of the piping under to neaten. Cut a piece of calico large enough to cover the back of the headboard with an allowance of 1.5cm (¾in) for turnings. Turn this under and attach the calico to the back of the headboard with gimp pins.

13 ◆ Finally attach the two pieces of planed timber to the back of the headboard, after lining up the holes at the top of the bed.

TARTAN APPEAL

A classic plaid makes an ideal top cover for this footstool — and it is also good practice for lining up patterns! This project introduces the technique of stitching.

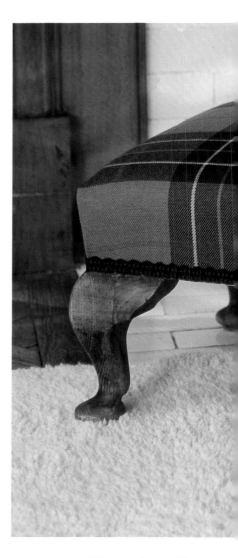

SIZE

Finished stool seat measures 32cm (12¾in) wide by 48cm (19¼in) long.

YOU WILL NEED

2.5m (102in) webbing

50cm (20in) of 315g (10oz) hessian

13mm fine and improved tacks

Stitching twine

1kg (2lb) black fibre

60cm (24in) scrim hessian

Card

1m (40in) linterfelt

60cm (24in) calico

50cm (20in) polyester wadding (batting)

60cm (24in) top cover fabric

10mm fine tacks

1.6m (64in) braid or gimp

Gimp pins

Fabric adhesive

Making up

1 ◆ If you are re-upholstering an old stool, strip and prepare the frame (see page 12). It is possible to buy stool frames or, as here, have a frame made by your local carpenter. This way you can have any shape or size you like!

2 ◆ Starting with the bare frame, working on a sturdy table or workbench, webb the top of the frame as on pages 14–15 using 13mm improved tacks. Use two strips of webbing on the short rails and three strips on the long rails.

3 ◆ Attach the hessian using 13mm fine tacks and make your bridles (see page 19). The bridles need to be fairly loose to accommodate stuffing to a thickness of approximately 10cm (4in). Stuff with black fibre.

4 ◆ Cut and attach the scrim hessian (see page 20) and then stitch your rolled edge. You will need to make two rows of blind stitching before making your rolled edge. Stay stitches are important here to ensure that all four corners remain square. As you stitch, regulate well (see page 21).

5 ◆ When you have finished stitching make shallow bridles and second stuff. Then cut four pieces of card and fit these to the four corners as shown. This will ensure a sharp edge for your corners.

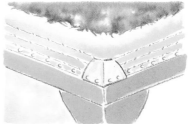

◆ *Fitting card corners*

6 ◆ Add two layers of linterfelt over the second stuffing, and attach the calico as on page 27 using 13mm fine tacks. When you are certain the calico is tight and the corners are neat, hammer home the tacks and trim the calico. Make sure your line of calico tacks are placed about 1cm (½ in) from the bottom of the frame to allow room for your top cover tacks to come below.

7 ◆ Lay a piece of polyester wadding (batting) over the calico. Then attach the top cover in the same way as the calico but place 10mm tacks near to the edge of the frame. Trim the fabric close to the tacks and cover the tacks with braid or gimp.

◆ *Tacking down the top cover*

Springs

*Springs can be used in addition to fibre
stuffing in some seats. The way you secure the springs
can make all the difference between a seat that is well sprung
and one that is uncomfortable!*

Attaching springs to the webbing

Using the right size and gauge of spring for the job in hand (see individual project), place the springs on the webbing, making sure that the knots of the springs face the centre of the frame. Thread a spring needle with a length of upholsterer's stitching twine. Starting with the spring furthest away from you, push the spring needle down through the webbing next to the spring and up again just outside the spring. Secure with an upholsterer's knot (see page 18). Make two further stitches in two different places in the webbing to attach the spring securely to the webbing. Continue until all the springs are attached to the webbing in the same way. Finish off with a double knot.

◆ *Securing springs to webbing (right)*

ATTACHING SPRINGS

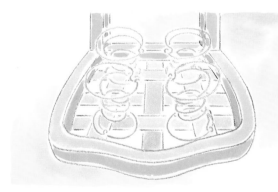

1 ◆ Position the springs on the webbing, ensuring that the knots of the springs face towards the centre of the webbing.

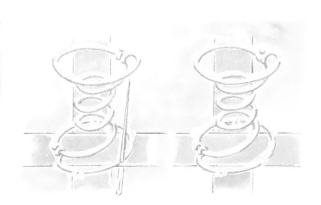

2 ◆ Starting with the spring furthest away from you, push a spring needle threaded with twine down through the webbing next to the spring, then up through the webbing over the base of the spring. Secure with an upholsterer's knot (see page 18).

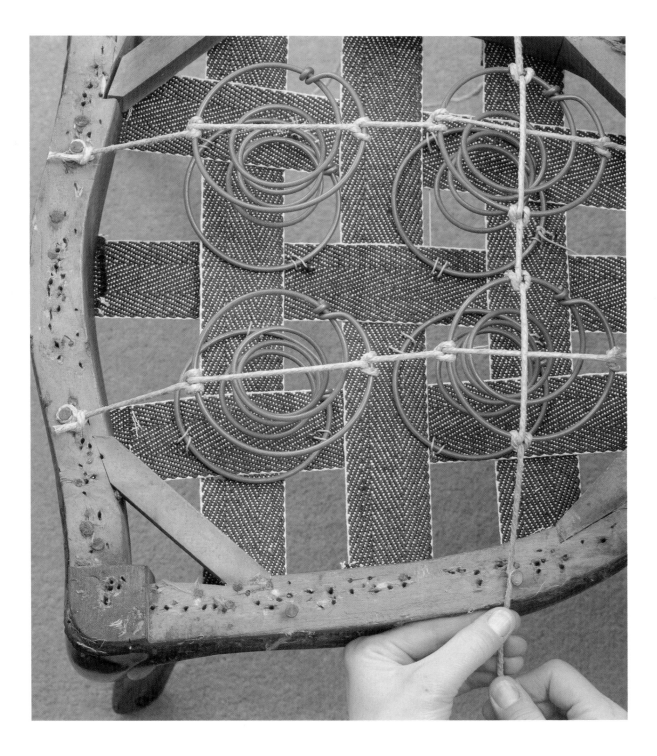

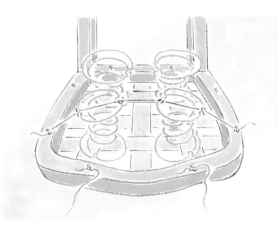

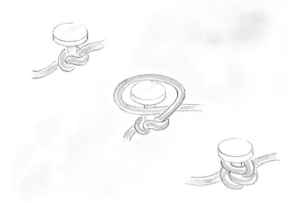

1 ◆ Hammer a tack into the frame in line with the centre of each row of springs. Tie a piece of laid cord to each of the tacks. The cord should be long enough to reach from one side of the frame to the other over the springs twice.

2 ◆ To attach the cord to the tacks, make a single knot at the end of a piece of laid cord and slip it over the head of a temporary tack. Pull it tight then make another knot around the tack and pull it tight again. Finally hammer the tack home to secure the knot. Repeat the process with the other tacks and pieces of laid cord on two sides.

Lashing the springs

The reason springs are lashed is to keep them upright and away from each other. They also need to be under tension. Using 16mm improved tacks, hammer one tack into the frame in line with the centre of each row of springs. Cut one piece of laid cord for each row of springs. Each piece should be long enough to reach from one side of the frame to the other over the springs twice. With a single knot at the end of one piece, slip it over one of the temporary tacks. Make another knot, pull it tight and hammer the tack home. Attach all the pieces of cord along the two adjoining rails in the same way.

Starting with the central row of springs, take the piece of cord opposite its nearest spring and make a clove hitch knot on the top coil at the point nearest the rail. Make sure that the spring leans slightly towards the rail after you have tied the knot. Then

make a half hitch knot on the top coil opposite the first knot. With the same piece of cord, make a half hitch on the top coil of the next spring and then another opposite that knot. Continue in this way until you reach the last spring in the row, compressing each spring about 2cm (¾ in) as you go.

Make your last knot a clove hitch, taking up the slack and attaching the cord to the temporary tack opposite as before. This last spring should lean towards the rail as did the first spring. Lash each row of springs in the same way, back to front and side to side. When completed, the shape of the sprung seat should look similar to the illustration opposite.

Lay a piece of 375g (12oz) hessian over the springs and attach it as described and illustrated opposite. The springs must now be attached to the hessian in the same way as they were to the webbing but this time using a large curved mattress needle.

clove hitch

half hitch

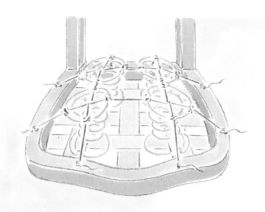

3 ◆ Taking the piece of cord opposite its nearest spring, make a clove hitch knot on the top coil at the point nearest the rail. The spring should lean slightly towards the rail. Then make a half hitch knot on the top coil of the same spring, opposite the first knot.

4 ◆ Continue knotting each spring in the same way, compressing each spring about 2cm (¾ in) as you go, until you reach the last spring in the row. Make the last knot a clove hitch and attach the cord to a temporary tack as before. This last spring should lean towards the rail. Lash each row of springs in the same way, front to back and side to side.

COVERING SPRINGS WITH HESSIAN

◆ Lay a piece of hessian over the springs and, turning up a 2.5cm (1in) hem along the back rail of the frame, attach it to the frame with 13mm fine tacks. Temporary tack at first, making sure that the hessian remains square. Pull the hessian towards you over the springs and tack it opposite the first tack. Then tack in the centre of the other two rails in the same way. Then pull the hessian tight from corner to corner, securing each corner with a tack. When you are sure the hessian is square and tight, hammer the tacks home firmly. Then trim the hessian and turn up the hem all the way around and tack down. Stitch the springs to the hessian using a large curved mattress needle, making three stitches per spring to secure.

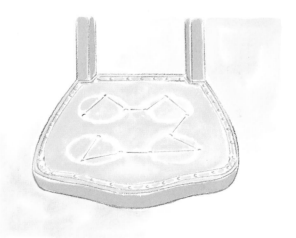

PERIOD ELEGANCE

The striped fabric gives this chair a contemporary
look without losing any of its Victorian elegance. This project
combines a stuff-over seat (one that is upholstered with
springs) with a pincushion chair back.

SIZE

Finished chair seat measures 44cm (17½in) wide and 40cm (16in) long. Finished chair back measures 33cm (13¼in) wide and 21cm (8¼in) long.

YOU WILL NEED

3m (5¾yd) webbing

13mm improved tacks

4 × 12.5cm (5in) coil springs, gauge 9 or 10

Stitching twine

16mm improved tacks

Laid cord

50cm (20in) of 375g (12oz) hessian

1.5kg (3lb) black fibre

60cm (24in) scrim hessian

13mm fine tacks

1.5m (62in) linterfelt

60cm (24in) calico

1m (40in) of 60g (2oz) polyester wadding (batting)

1m (40in) top cover fabric

10mm fine tacks

1.6m (64in) braid or gimp

Gimp pins

Fabric adhesive

50cm (20in) bottom cloth

CHAIR SEAT

1 ◆ Strip and prepare the frame (see page 12). Usually, the older the chair, the more preparation will be needed. This chair was stripped, filled with sawdust and wood glue and the joints were then re-glued and cramped.

2 ◆ You may find it easier to work on a pair of trestles for this job; otherwise use a sturdy table or work bench and turn the chair upside-down on it. Webb the chair on the underside as on pages 14–15 using three pieces from back to front and three pieces from side to side, positioned as shown below.

3 ◆ Turn the chair the right way up and place four coil springs in the seat on top of the webbing. The gauge of the springs depends on the hardness of the seat required – the higher the gauge the softer the seat. Secure the springs to the webbing (see page 46).

4 ◆ Lash the springs as on page 48. You should finish up with a seat that is domed in the middle and slopes away to the sides.

5 ◆ Place a piece of hessian over the springs and tack it down using 13mm improved tacks. Then attach the top of the springs to the hessian using stitching twine and a large curved mattress needle.

6 ◆ Starting at the back of the seat, make bridle stitches, working from back to front. The stitches need to be looser around the edge of the seat where the springs slope away, and tighter at the top. The bridles will then be able to accommodate more stuffing around the edge of the seat.

7 ◆ Stuff the bridles with black fibre (see page 19). Make sure you stuff up very firmly around the edge of the seat to bring the sides of the seat level with the top.

8 ◆ Cut the piece of scrim large enough to cover the stuffing and attach it using 13mm fine tacks. Cut for the two obstructions (see page 34) and, using the flat part of your regulator, tuck the scrim down and around the obstructions once you have cut away the excess. Tack the scrim home once you are sure that it is taut and the stuffing feels firm underneath. Finish the corners neatly.

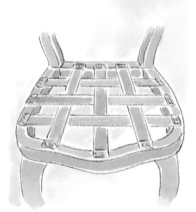

◆ *Positioning the webbing*

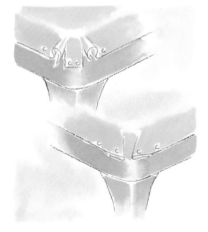

◆ *Neatening the corners*

9 ◆ Make about six to eight large stay stitches (see page 21). Then start to blind stitch. For this chair two rows of blind stitching before you make your rolled edge will be enough. Regulate well between stitches to bring the stuffing towards the edge. Then make your rolled edge, taking care to regulate well at the corners to make sure they remain upright and do not slope backwards. You now have the basic shape of your seat.

10 ◆ Make another set of bridles, shallow this time, and second stuff with black fibre. Then lay in position two layers of linterfelt, and attach the calico. Cut for obstructions and finish the corners as you did the scrim.

11 ◆ Lay a piece of polyester wadding (batting) over the calico and attach the top cover as you did the calico using 10mm fine tacks.

12 ◆ Glue on a suitable braid to cover the tacks. Then finish the seat by attaching a piece of bottom cloth to the underside of the chair to cover the webbing.

CHAIR BACK
1 ◆ Lay the chair on its back and place an old cushion or folded blanket underneath it to support the frame. Cut a piece of top cover fabric large enough to cover the back panel plus an allowance of 1.5cm (⅝in) all around. Lay this on the panel with the right side of the fabric facing downwards, making sure the pattern on the fabric is square. Now, using 10mm fine tacks, tack the fabric to the rebated edge, starting with temporary tacks on the centre of each

rail. Fill in with more tacks, working from the centre of each rail outwards. Do not trim the fabric at this stage.

2 ◆ Cut a piece of hessian the same size as the top cover fabric and attach this over the top cover fabric in the same way. Turn the fabric and hessian over together and tack this down, making a neat edge all around.

3 ◆ Place two layers of linterfelt on top of the hessian. This should be the same size as the panel but fritter away the edge by pulling small pieces off with your fingers (see below). Now place a piece of polyester wadding (batting) over the linterfelt and tuck this under all around the edges.

4 ◆ Cut a piece of top cover fabric about 3cm (1¼in) larger than the panel and lay this over the wadding (batting), keeping the pattern square. Place three temporary tacks (10mm fine) in the rail nearest you. Drawing the fabric away from you and smoothing

with your hands as you go, place three more temporary tacks in the opposite rail. Do the same on the side rails. Now fill in with more tacks, drawing the fabric away from the centre and towards the corners at the same time. This should prevent 'tack ties' appearing. Pull the fabric tight so that the stuffing feels firm to the touch underneath. Hammer the tacks home firmly and trim the fabric. If the frame is very delicate, use gimp pins to attach the top cover. Finish off by covering the tacks with braid or gimp (see below).

This type of chair back is called a 'pincushion' and the same method of upholstery can be used for stuffing 'pincushion seats'. In the case of seats or chair backs larger than this one, you will need to webb before the hessian is put on. Use three webbs each way for seats but chair backs may only need one or two strips to give enough support.

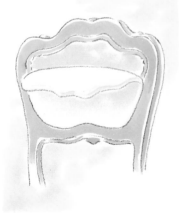

◆ *Positioning the linterfelt*

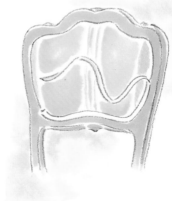

◆ *Attaching braid to the chair back*

LADDER STITCH

*Ladder stitch is used to join two pieces of fabric
that butt together with an invisible line of stitching. It is also
known as slip stitch.*

Fold in the raw edges of the fabric and butt the two pieces together. Working from the right side of the fabric, and using a 7.5cm (3in) curved needle, make a small stitch just to the right of the start of the seam and secure it with an upholsterer's knot (see page 18). Now make a stitch through the fold of the fabric back to the start of the seam. This should hide the upholsterer's knot. Working from right to left, make your first stitch by inserting the needle into the opposite fold and bringing it out a stitch length later still in the opposite fold. Start the next stitch a thread or two back from the last, in the first fold. In this way, as you pull the thread tight between stitches it will be concealed. When you reach the end of the seam, finish with a French knot (see page 23) to secure. Ladder stitch can also be used for sewing cord onto seat covers or chair backs – simply take your needle through the cord as you stitch.

◆ *Joining fabric with ladder stitch (right)*

LADDER STITCHING

1 ◆ Using a 7.5cm (3in) curved needle, make a small stitch just to the right of the start of the seam and secure it with an upholsterer's knot (see page 18).

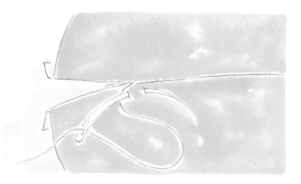

2 ◆ Make a stitch through the fold of the fabric back to the start of the seam to hide the knot.

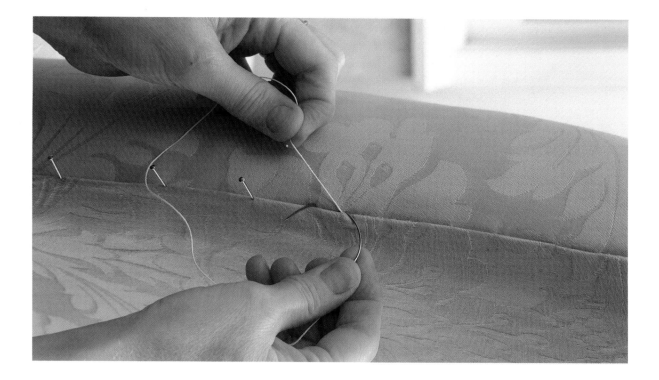

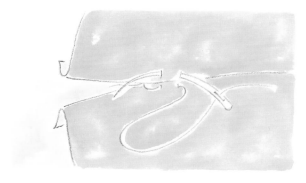

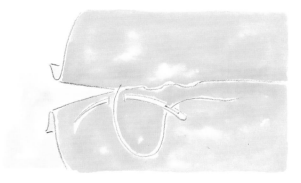

3 ◆ Working from right to left, insert the needle into the opposite fold and bring it out a stitch length later, still in the opposite fold of fabric.

4 ◆ Bring the needle a thread or two back from the last stitch and make another stitch in the first fold of fabric. As you pull the thread tight, the stitches will be concealed. Continue making stitches on alternate folds until you reach the end of the seam.

DECORATIVE DAMASK

*With this small bedroom chair you will be able
to use most of the upholstery techniques you have already learned
and add a new and very useful skill to your repertoire –
ladder stitching.*

SIZE

Finished chair seat
measures 55cm (22in) wide
and 55cm (22in) long.

YOU WILL NEED

4 zigzag springs cut to size
and 8 clips

60cm (24in) of 375g (12oz)
hessian

13mm fine tacks

Stitching twine

2–2.5kg (4–5lb) black fibre

60cm (24in) scrim hessian

2m (2¼yd) linterfelt

60cm (24in) calico

2m (2¼yd) top cover fabric

Waxed thread or button
thread

1.5m (62in) of 125g (4oz)
polyester wadding
(batting)

1m (40in) bottom cloth

3.5m (142in) cord to match
fringe

2m (2¼yd) bullion fringe,
21cm (8½in) long

CHAIR SEAT

1 ◆ Strip and prepare the chair
(see page 12). You may be able to
leave the springs intact – they do
not often need replacing. If they
do, ask your local upholsterer to
cut four springs the right size and
secure them to the frame using
special clips (see below).

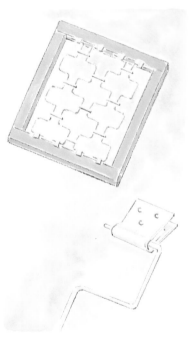

◆ *Zigzag springs attached with clips*

2 ◆ Cover the springs with hessian
using 13mm fine tacks. At the
back of the chair take the hessian
under the bottom rail of the back
and tack it down on the other side
of the back rail of the seat. Cut for
the obstructions at the back (see
page 34). Attach the hessian to
the springs in a few places using a
spring needle and stitching twine.

3 ◆ Make fairly loose bridles to
accommodate stuffing to a thickness of 8cm (3¼in) and stuff up
with black fibre. Fill any gaps and
make sure the stuffing is thick and
firm. The stuffing should fill the
gap between the bottom rail of
the back and seat.

4 ◆ Attach a piece of scrim hessian
using 13mm fine tacks over the
black fibre. Cut for the two back
obstructions and finish the corners neatly. Attach the scrim to
the back rail in the same way as
the hessian. Place about four
large stay stitches in the seat and
then make one row of blind
stitches before making your roll
edge. This should be fairly fat and
protrude over the edge by about
1cm (½in).

5 ◆ Make another set of shallow
bridles and second stuff with

black fibre to fill the depression left after stitching. Use two layers of linterfelt to cover the fibre, the first layer stopping just short of the rolled edge and the second covering it completely.

6 ◆ Cut a piece of calico large enough to cover the top of the seat plus about 8cm (3¼ in) all around. Cover the linterfelt with the calico. Secure the calico on the front of the chair just below the rolled edge with three skewers. Then smooth and press with your hand towards the back and place three temporary tacks (13mm fine) in the back rail of the seat. Now cut for the two back obstructions. Secure the calico on the two sides with three more skewers on each side. Smoothing and pressing as you go and working from the centre outwards, insert more skewers until the calico is secure all around the front of the seat (see below). Pull the calico tight at the back and tack down. Stitch around the front of the seat using a blind stitch (see below).

7 ◆ Cut a piece of top cover fabric 8cm (3¼ in) larger all around than the top of the seat. Attach this in exactly the same way as the calico.

8 ◆ Cut a strip of top cover fabric 12cm (4¾ in) deep and wide enough to reach right around the front of the chair. You will probably have to machine an extra piece of fabric on each side to make the strip long enough. Turn over 2cm (¾ in) at the top and find the centre of the fabric and the centre of the front of the seat. Starting from the middle outwards, secure this strip of fabric just above your stitching line on the seat with skewers as shown below.

9 ◆ Using a 7.5cm (3in) curved mattress needle and waxed or button thread, ladder stitch this to the top cover of the seat (see page 54). Lift the skirt and place two layers of polyester wadding (batting) cut to size underneath. Then tack the bottom edge underneath the chair. Cut the fabric around the legs and tack down. Finish the seat by attaching a piece of bottom cloth on the underside of the frame to cover the springs.

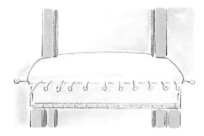

◆ *Securing calico with skewers*

◆ *Blind stitching*

◆ *Securing top cover fabric with skewers*

CHAIR BACK

1 ◆ Lay the chair on its back and place two strips of webbing from the top rail to the bottom rail and one strip from one side rail to the other, approximately in the centre of the back. Use 13mm fine tacks to tack the webbs in place (see page 15).

2 ◆ Cover this webbing with a piece of hessian tacked in place with 13mm fine tacks. Then make fairly tight bridles, working from top to bottom, and stuff with curly black fibre.

3 ◆ Cover the fibre with two layers of linterfelt, taking care not to take the linterfelt over the edge of the frame. Now cover the linterfelt with a layer of polyester wadding (batting) but this time take the wadding (batting) over the edge of the frame. Secure the wadding (batting) with a few tacks all the way around to keep the stuffing in place. Turn the chair the right way up.

4 ◆ Cut a piece of top cover fabric large enough to cover the stuffing and the frame of the chair back, allowing enough fabric to tuck down through the gap between the seat and back so that you can tack onto the back rail of the seat. Lay the fabric on the back, making sure the pattern is square and centred and that it matches the pattern on the seat.

5 ◆ Temporary tack three 13mm fine tacks on the top rail. Temporary tack the fabric to the outside of the back rail of the seat, smoothing and pressing as you go. Cut for the two bottom obstructions (see page 34).

6 ◆ Then temporary tack the fabric to the back of the two side rails in the same way, smoothing and pressing as you go. Work from the centre outwards on each rail, first the top rail, then the two side rails, and finally the bottom rail. Finish the corners neatly (see page 36). When you are sure that the fabric is tight, even, and firm to the touch, hammer the tacks home firmly all around and trim the fabric close to the line of tacks.

7 ◆ You are now ready to finish the outer back. Take a piece of calico or bottom cloth the right size to cover the outer back with no turnings. Attach this to the outer back about 1cm (½in) from the edge all the way around. Cut a piece of top cover fabric large enough to cover the back plus an allowance of 1.5cm (⅝in) for turnings. Starting at the top, turn

◆ *Pinned chair back*

under 1.5cm (⅝in) of the fabric and pin this to the top edge. Space your pins about 2cm (¾in) apart. Take the fabric under the base of the chair and tack in position. Then pin each side. Before you start to stitch, the back of the chair should look like the diagram below. Then, using a 7.5cm (3in) curved mattress needle and waxed or button thread, ladder stitch all the way around (see page 54). Cut the fabric for the legs, turn under and secure in place with a gimp pin.

8 ◆ You can now ladder stitch your decorative cord over the two seams you have made both under the rolled edge and around the outer back. Wrap a small piece of sticky tape around the cord before you start stitching it in place to prevent it unravelling. Use a 7.5cm (3in) cording needle and a length of waxed or button thread for sewing on the cord. Tuck the end of the cord in between your stitches on the outer back to hide the end when you stitch the cord around the front of the chair. When you stitch the cord to the outer back, the end will be covered by the bullion fringe.

9 ◆ Sew the bullion fringe around the base of the chair so that the chair legs are hidden. Start by turning over one end of the fringe and secure it with a gimp pin in the centre of the outer back. Pin the fringe in position before you start sewing to make sure it is level. When you have finished sewing, turn the end under and secure with a gimp pin.

DEEP BUTTONING

*Attaching rows of buttons is a traditional method
of upholstery which adds depth and shape to furniture. Your local
upholsterer will usually be happy to cover buttons for you in your
own fabric at a small cost.*

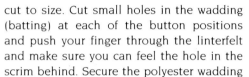

Laying out the button positions

When the back of your piece of furniture has
been stuffed and stitched with a rolled edge,
you will be ready to mark out the button
positions on the scrim.

Buttons are normally laid out in alternate rows so
that the pleats form a diamond pattern between the
buttons. The buttons must be arranged in straight
lines and spaced equally. Find the centre of the back
and mark it with tailor's chalk. When you start to lay
out your buttons, place skewers in the approximate
positions you think the buttons should be. Use the
diagram opposite as a guide. It is important to
remember at this stage that the distance between the
bottom row of buttons and the seat should be
slightly larger than the distance between the top row
of buttons to the top of the back.

When you are happy with the position of your
skewers, remove each one and mark the position of
each by making a small hole in the scrim. Take the
regulator and, making sure you are holding it level,
push it through each hole in the scrim to the hessian
at the back and mark each point in the hessian with a
felt-tip pen. Now make a diagram of the button
positions on a piece of paper, indicating the distances
between the buttons.

Lay the first layer of linterfelt over the scrim. Make
holes in the linterfelt with your finger at each of the
button positions so that you can feel the hole in the
scrim behind. Do this with two further layers of
linterfelt. Finish stuffing by covering the linterfelt
with a layer of 280g (9oz) polyester wadding (batting)

cut to size. Cut small holes in the wadding
(batting) at each of the button positions
and push your finger through the linterfelt
and make sure you can feel the hole in the
scrim behind. Secure the polyester wadding
(batting) with a few 13mm fine tacks in the top and
side rails to stop the stuffing moving around as you
are buttoning.

Marking out the top cover

To calculate the size of the top cover, measure from
the top rail, over the stuffing, and under the bottom
rail. Add an extra 2cm (¾in) for each row of buttons.
Now measure from side to side and add an extra 4cm
(1½in) for each row of buttons. Cut out the top cover
fabric to this size and lay it wrong side uppermost.
Mark the centre.

Measure from the back rail over the stuffing and
deep into the nearest buttonhole of the first row.
Measure this distance from the top of the fabric and
draw a straight chalk line across the fabric at this
point. From your diagram of button positions take
the measurement between the vertical buttons and
add an allowance of 2cm (¾in). Draw another line for
the next row of buttons at this distance from the first
and repeat for each row of buttons. Now mark the
position of the buttons on these lines using the
measurements on your diagram and adding an
allowance of 4cm (1½in) between the buttons. Start
from the centre button and work outwards.

◆ *Marking button positions (right)*

MARKING BUTTON POSITIONS

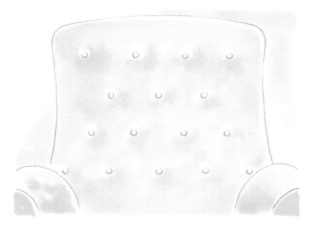

♦ Arrange buttons in straight lines, leaving equal spaces between each, as shown. The distance between the bottom row of buttons and the seat should be slightly larger than the distance between the top row of buttons and the top of the chair back.

MARKING THE TOP COVER FABRIC

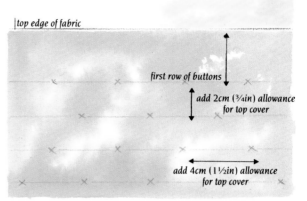

top edge of fabric

first row of buttons

add 2cm (¾in) allowance for top cover

add 4cm (1½in) allowance for top cover

♦ Mark the positions of the buttons on chalk lines on the top cover, following the measurements you have taken, and adding an allowance of 2cm (¾in) for each vertical row of buttons, and 4cm (1½in) for each row of buttons from side to side.

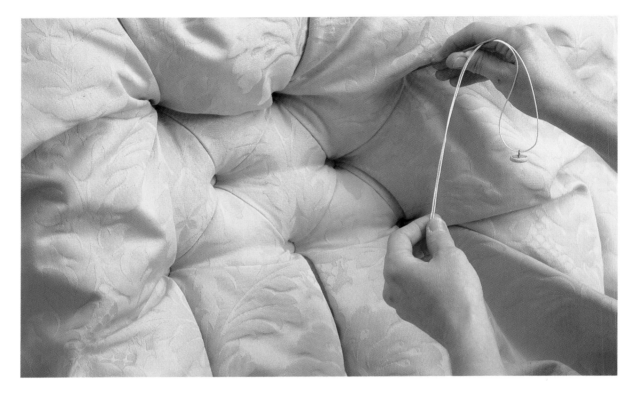

Deep Buttoning

For the technique of deep buttoning you will need a 30cm (12in) double pointed needle, the correct number of buttons, an equal number of 40cm (16in) lengths of nylon tufting twine and an equal number of small pieces of webbing.

Thread a button onto a piece of twine and then thread the two ends of the twine through the eye of the needle together. Start with the centre button of the bottom row and match the correct mark on the fabric with the correct button position on the chair.

Take the needle through the fabric and then the stuffing and bring it out at the corresponding mark on the back hessian. Pull the threads through and, placing a small piece of rolled-up webbing between the threads, make an upholsterer's knot (see page 18) and pull fairly tight. Repeat this with all the buttons on the bottom row and the next row up. Make folds or pleats between the buttons as you go. You may find it helpful to use the flat end of your regulator here. All

◆ *Stitching buttons to the top cover fabric (above)*

the folds should face downwards. Continue with each row in the same way until all the buttons are in place and the pleats are neat.

Now take the fabric over the top and side rails, pull tightly and temporary tack. Take care to fold the fabric in pleats from each button to the edge of the fabric. Cut for obstructions in the normal way (see page 00).

Now fold the fabric back from the bottom row of buttons. Cut slits in the polyester wadding (batting) in straight lines from the buttons to the seat. Take the fabric back over the wadding (batting) and under the bottom rail between the back and the seat. Make your folds and ease the pleats into the crevices.

When you are happy with the position of the pleats, pull the fabric fairly tightly and hammer the tacks home. Then hammer the tacks home on the back and side rails. Finally pull the knots tight at the back of the chair and tie off with granny knots.

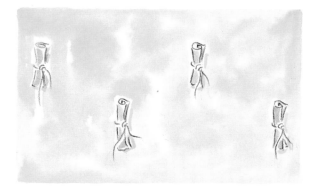

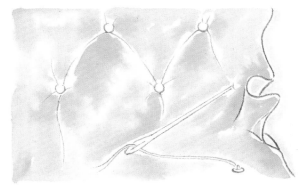

1 ◆ Starting with the centre button on each row, take a needle double-threaded with tufting twine and a button through the fabric and stuffing and bring it out at the corresponding mark on the back hessian. Pull the two threads through, place a small piece of rolled-up webbing between the threads, then make an upholsterer's knot and pull tight.

2 ◆ Make neat folds or pleats in the top cover fabric between the buttons as you go. All the folds should face downwards. Continue with each row in the same way until all the buttons are attached.

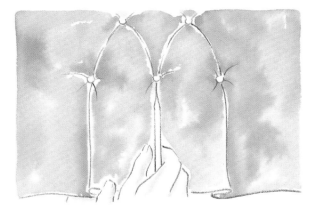

3 ◆ Temporary tack the top cover fabric to the top and side rails. Fold the fabric back from the bottom row of buttons and cut straight slits in the wadding (batting) from the buttons to the seat. Then take the fabric back over the wadding (batting), easing the pleats into the crevices with a regulator.

4 ◆ When you are happy with the position of the pleats, pull the fabric tightly and hammer the tacks home all around the frame. Pull the knots tight at the back of the chair and tie off the tufting twine with granny knots to secure.

BUTTONED UP

This chaise longue may seem rather
ambitious at first glance but, by adapting the techniques you have
already learned and by adding a new one – deep buttoning
– you should feel confident in tackling it.

SIZE

Finished chaise longue measures 70cm (28in) wide, 180cm (72in) long and 90cm (36in) high.

YOU WILL NEED

27m (30¼yd) webbing

16mm and 13mm improved tacks

12 × 10cm (4in) arm springs, 12 gauge

Stitching twine

3m (3¼yd) 375g (12oz) hessian

8–9kg (16–18lb) black fibre

3m (3¼yd) scrim hessian

10m (11¼yd) linterfelt

3m (3¼yd) of 280g (9oz), and 2m (2¼yd) of 60g (2oz) polyester wadding (batting)

13mm and 10mm fine tacks

5.5m (6¼yd) top cover fabric

Nylon tufting twine

57 fabric-covered buttons

24 × 17.5cm (7in) seat springs, 9 or 10 gauge

Laid cord

3m (3¼yd) calico

50cm (20in) square of buckram

Fabric adhesive

Key tassel and rosette

1m (40in) matching cord

Gimp pins

6m (6¾yd) braid or gimp

2m (2¼yd) bottom cloth

THE ARM

1 ◆ Starting with a bare frame, having stripped the old upholstery and prepared the frame by filling any tack holes and repairing any loose joints (see page 12), place the chaise longue on two sturdy trestles. Working from one side of the frame to the other, attach seven pieces of webbing with 16mm improved tacks, placing them approximately 4–5cm (1½–2in) apart (see page 14).

2 ◆ Position twelve 10cm (4in) springs on the webbing in four rows of three springs, ensuring that the knots of the springs face the centre of the frame. Then attach these to the webbing in the usual way (see page 46). Lash the springs in the same way as before, but this time using stitching twine instead of laid cord (see page 48).

3 ◆ Cover the springs with hessian using 13mm improved tacks to secure and attach the springs to the hessian with a spring needle and stitching twine.

4 ◆ Working from top to bottom of the arm, make fairly deep bridles all over the hessian to accommodate stuffing to a thickness of 10–12.5cm (4–5in). Tuck handfuls of black fibre under and around each bridle stitch, again working from top to bottom of the arm. Make sure the stuffing is even and that there are no gaps when you have finished (see page 19).

5 ◆ Cover the stuffing with scrim using 13mm improved tacks (see page 20). Take your time to adjust the scrim to the shape of the frame, making sure that you keep the scrim square as you work. Temporary tack the scrim along each rail. When you are happy with the shape and the scrim is taut and straight, tack home. Place several large stay stitches in the scrim to hold the stuffing firm and square while you make the stitched edge. Make two rows of blind stitching and one row of topstitching to make your rolled edge (see page 24).

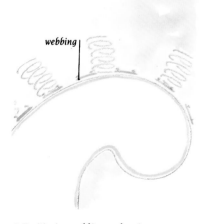

◆ *Positioning webbing and springs*

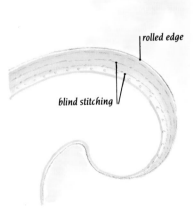

◆ *Making the rolled edge*

13cm (5¼in)

7.5cm (3in)

◆ *Marking button positions on the scrim of the arm*

13cm + 4cm = 17cm
(5¼in + 1½in = 6¾in)

7.5cm + 2cm = 9.5cm
(3in + ¾in = 3¾in)

◆ *Marking button positions on the top cover fabric of the arm*

6 ◆ You are now ready to mark out your button positions on the arm. Using the diagram below as a guide, place skewers in the scrim where you think the buttons should be and mark accordingly (see page 60). Now make a diagram of the button positions.

7 ◆ Place three layers of linterfelt onto the scrim, making holes in each layer where each button should be (see page 60). Place one layer of 280g (9oz) polyester wadding (batting) over the linterfelt and mark holes in this at the button positions. Secure the wadding (batting) in place over the linterfelt with 13mm fine tacks on the top and side rails.

8 ◆ Cut a piece of top cover fabric 110cm (44in) wide × 160cm (66in) deep. Mark the back of the top cover using your diagram and adding the necessary allowances.

9 ◆ Using a 30cm (12in) double pointed needle and tufting twine, insert the buttons two rows at a time, starting with the centre button in the bottom row and working upwards (see page 63). When

tying the upholsterer's knot for each button, do not pull the twine too tight – pull just enough for the button to sit deep but still be visible from the front. If you pull too tight the button might disappear into the wadding (batting)! Take your time arranging the pleats between the buttons, making sure that the pleats always face downwards.

10 ◆ Arrange the pleats from the buttons to the edge of the fabric and temporary tack to the centre of the front rail with 13mm fine tacks. Cut for the obstructions where the back meets the arm and temporary tack to the back rail. Now pleat the fabric and temporary tack to the top rail. This will be awkward to do so only put in as many tacks as you need to hold the pleats. Fold the fabric back at the bottom and cut the polyester wadding (batting) from each of the bottom buttons to the base. Fold the fabric back, taking it under the bottom rail and arrange the pleats. Do not tack home at this stage. Return to the front rail

and temporary tack some more, working from the centre to the base first. Then work from the centre upwards around the scroll, arranging the pleats carefully as you go. They should all go in the same direction. When you are satisfied with the pleats, hammer the tacks home on the front and back rails but leave the top and bottom rails for the time being. Trim the fabric if necessary. Tie off the button threads at the back with granny knots to secure them.

◆ *Arranging pleats around the scroll*

THE BACK

1 ◆ Lay the chaise on its back on a flat surface. Cut a piece of hessian the size of the back plus 12mm (½in) for turning. Tack this in place using 13mm fine tacks (see page 16).

2 ◆ Make bridles to accommodate stuffing to the thickness of 7.5–10cm (3–4in), working from top to bottom. Place the chaise back on the trestles. Stuff firmly with fibre. Now cover the stuffing carefully with scrim using 13mm fine tacks. Cut the scrim roughly to shape before you start. It is very important at this stage to keep the scrim square so start with temporary tacks at the top and bottom and work from the centre at the top outwards. Take care to follow the shape of the frame and place your tacks far enough away from the rebate to leave enough room for the top cover tacks. Put in several large stay stitches before you stitch. Now stitch two rows of blind stitching, finishing off with a rolled edge.

3 ◆ Following the diagram below, mark the button positions with skewers. When you are happy with them, remove the skewers and mark with tailor's chalk (see page 60). Lay two layers of linterfelt over the scrim, making holes in each layer at the button positions. Then place one layer of 280g (9oz) polyester wadding (batting) on the linterfelt and cut small holes in the wadding (batting) at the button positions (see page 60). Secure the polyester wadding (batting) with 13mm fine tacks.

4 ◆ Cut two pieces of top cover fabric to cover the back: the larger piece should be 135cm (54in) wide and 75cm (30in) deep, and the smaller piece should be 55cm (22in) wide and 45cm (18in) deep. Before you cut, make sure that you line up the fabric so that the pattern matches from the base upwards. Now mark the back of the fabric using your diagram and making the necessary allowances (see page 60).

5 ◆ Starting with the uppermost

button, attach the buttons (see page 63) two rows at a time and neatening the pleats as you go. Where the fabric joins, simply fold the fabric as you insert the button. Make sure the pattern of the fabric matches.

6 ◆ Lay the chaise on its back again. Arrange the pleats from the buttons to the edge of the fabric along the top edge. Temporary tack to the top rail with 13mm fine tacks, starting at the centre and working outwards, cutting away the excess fabric as you work. When you are satisfied with the pleating, tack home along the top rail and trim the fabric. Now turn the chaise the right way up and fold the fabric back from the bottom row of buttons. Make slits in the polyester wadding (batting) from the buttons to the base. Take the fabric back under the bottom rail, arranging the pleats as you do so. Do not tack down at this stage. Tie off the button threads at the back with granny knots to secure them.

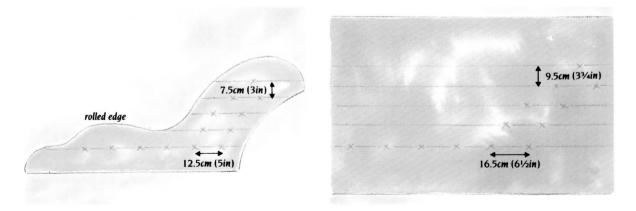

◆ *Marking button positions on the scrim of the back*

◆ *Marking button positions on the top cover fabric of the back*

THE SEAT

1 ◆ Turn the chaise upside-down, either on the floor or on your trestles. Using 16mm improved tacks, webb the frame (see page 14) with 15 strips of webbing back to front and six strips lengthwise.

2 ◆ Turn the chaise the right way up and attach 24 × 17.5cm (7in) springs to the webbing using stitching twine and a spring needle (see page 46). Arrange the springs in three rows of eight. Lash the springs (see page 48) with laid cord, working from back to front first and then from side to side. When you have finished, the shape of the seat should be level on the top and slope away to the sides.

3 ◆ Cover the springs with hessian (see page 16) and attach each spring to the hessian in three places, using a spring needle and stitching twine.

4 ◆ Make bridle stitches (see page 19) working from back to front. These should be fairly tight on the top of the seat and looser at the front and sides to accommodate more stuffing. Stuff firmly with black fibre, ensuring that there are no gaps and that the stuffing feels thick and firm. The sides should now be level with the top.

5 ◆ Cut a piece of scrim large enough to cover the stuffing, lay this over the stuffing and cut roughly to shape, allowing enough around the edge to turn over. Temporary tack back and front and side to side using 13mm improved tacks and cut for the obstructions (see page 34). Following the shape of the frame and working on each rail from the centre outwards, temporary tack around the seat, keeping the scrim straight and square. Finish off the rounded corners by making several small pleats. Hammer home and trim when you are happy with the shape of the seat. Working from side to side, place two rows of large stay stitches in the seat.

6 ◆ Make two rows of blind stitches before stitching your rolled edge. Regulate well as you stitch. Now make shallow bridles all over the scrim, working from front to back. Stuff with black fibre to fill the depression left by the stitching. Lay two layers of linter-felt over the second stuffing, making sure that the linterfelt covers the rolled edge.

7 ◆ Cut a piece of calico large enough to cover the seat and attach this using 13mm fine tacks (see page 27). Temporary tack on the front and back rails first then cut for the obstructions. Now, smoothing and pressing as you go, pull the calico taut and temporary tack again at the front and sides, working from the centre outwards each time. Keep removing the tacks and pulling the calico tighter. Finish the rounded corners with small pleats as you did the scrim. When you are happy that the calico is as tight as you can make it, hammer the tacks home and trim.

8 ◆ Cover the calico with one layer of 60g (2oz) polyester wadding (batting). Cut a piece of top cover fabric 137cm (54in) wide and 110cm (44in) deep and two further pieces 40cm (16in) wide and 110cm (44in) deep. These two smaller pieces need to be machine stitched on each side of the main piece of fabric so make sure when you are cutting out that any pattern will match. Match the pattern and join the pieces together. Now cover the polyester wadding (batting) with the top cover, lining up the centre of the pattern on the back with the centre of the pattern on the seat. Attach the top cover fabric with 10mm fine tacks in the same way as the calico – temporary tack at first and finish the corners with several small pleats. Hammer the tacks home and trim the fabric.

Finishing off

1 ◆ Return to the back of the chaise and tack the base of the fabric covering the back to the back rail with 13mm fine tacks. Make sure as you do this that the pleats are straight. Do the same to the base of the fabric covering the arm. Hammer the tacks home and trim the fabric.

2 ◆ Turn the chaise upside-down and tack the fabric to the top rail of the arm, making sure that the pleats are straight. Hammer the tacks home and trim the fabric. Turn the chaise the right way up again.

3 ◆ Cut a piece of calico large enough to cover the outer back and tack this in place using 10mm fine tacks. Place your tacks approximately 12mm (½in) from the top cover line to allow room for the top cover tacks. Hammer the tacks home and trim.

4 ◆ Cut a piece of fabric large enough to cover the outer back of the chaise. Attach this in the same way as you did the calico with 10mm fine tacks. To keep the fabric straight as you tack, start with three temporary tacks at the top and then take the fabric under the chaise and temporary tack there. Now work from the centre to the sides, tacking top and bottom as you go. Finish off by tacking the sides. Hammer the tacks home and trim. Where the arm joins the outer back you may need to pin and ladder stitch (see page 54).

5 ◆ Cut a piece of calico the right size to cover the outer arm. Tack this to the edge of the side rails and under the base of the chaise. Pin and ladder stitch the top edge. Now cut a piece of top cover fabric large enough to cover the outer arm plus 2.5cm (1in) for turnings. Attach this to the outer arm by tacking the fabric to the front and bottom rails and pinning and ladder stitching along the top edge and back rail.

6 ◆ Now you need to cover the scroll of the arm by making a facing. We have used a fairly elaborate method using cord and a tassel. Make a paper pattern of the bottom half of the scroll (marked A in the diagram below, and extending to the dotted line). Cut a piece of card or stiff buckram to this shape. Lay a piece of 60g (2oz) polyester wadding (batting) over this shape. Cut a piece of fabric the same shape plus a 2cm (¾in) allowance and lay this over the top. Take the fabric over the edge and stick down with fabric adhesive. Secure by pinning and ladder stitching.

7 ◆ Now cut a 22.5cm (9in) circle of card or stiff buckram. Cut a strip of top cover fabric measuring 12.5 × 75cm (5 × 30in) and stick this around the edge of the back of the circle with fabric adhesive, turning over the two ends. Place the circle on the scroll of the chaise, covering the top edge of the lower half of the scroll. Secure with four 13mm fine tacks. Now place a 22.5cm (9in) circle of polyester wadding (batting) over the buckram and bring the fabric forward over the wadding (batting). Pleat the fabric into the centre and secure each pleat with a 13mm fine tack. Keep the tacks in a tight circle at the centre. Hammer the tacks home and trim the fabric. Ladder stitch around the edge of the circle and ladder stitch the tassel and rosette in the centre. Sew the cord around the outer edge of the scroll, securing at each end with a gimp pin.

8 ◆ Cover the raw edges of fabric with gimp or braid (see page 29). Finally turn the chaise upside-down and cover the webbing with a bottom cloth.

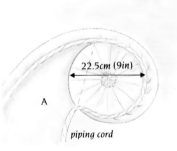

◆ *Pleating top cover fabric over the circle of wadding (batting)*

SUPPLIERS

Tools and upholstery materials supplied by:

Traditions,
259 Ewell Road,
Surbiton,
Surrey KT6 7AA
Tel: 0181-390 4472

Trimmings supplied by:

Wemyss Houlès,
40 Newman Street,
London W1P 3PA
Tel: 0171-255 3305

Henry Newberry & Co Ltd,
18 Newman Street,
London W1P 4AB
Tel: 0171-636 5970

Fabric for the dining chair (page 30) supplied by:

Designers Guild,
227 Kings Road,
London SW3
Tel: 0171-351 5775

Fabric for the screen (page 38) supplied by:

G.P. & J. Baker Ltd,
PO Box 30,
West End Road,
High Wycombe,
Buckinghamshire HP11 2QD
Tel: 01494 471166

Dovedale Fabrics,
Kew Ltd,
13 Mount Road,
Feltham,
Middlesex TW13 6AR
Tel: 0181-893 4222

Fabric for the headboard (page 40) supplied by:

Zoffany Ltd,
Talbot House,
17 Church Street,
Rickmansworth,
Hertfordshire WD3 1DE
Tel: 01923 710680

Fabric for the stool (page 44), Victorian chair (page 50) and chaise longue (page 64) supplied by:

Romo Fabrics
Romo Ltd,
Lowmoor Road,
Kirkby in Ashfield,
Nottingham NG17 7DE
Tel: 01623 750005

Fabric for the bedroom chair (page 56) supplied by:

Warner Fabrics PLC,
Bradbourne Drive,
Tilbrook,
Milton Keynes MK7 8BE
Tel: 01908 366900

Index

ACKNOWLEDGEMENTS

Our grateful thanks to: Sheena Davies, Julie Carter, Vivien
Thornton, Elizabeth Jewell and Graham Lynn.